# THE 4TH GRADE SPELLING WORKBOOK

## 95+ GAMES AND PUZZLES TO IMPROVE SPELLING SKILLS

Rae Pritchett M.ED., CAGS

Illustrations by Joel and Ashley Selby

CALLISTO PUBLISHING

Published by Callisto Publishing LLC C/O Sourcebooks LLC

P.O. Box 4410, Naperville, Illinois 60567-4410

(630) 961-3900

callistopublishing.com

This product conforms to all applicable CPSC and CPSIA standards.

Source of Production: Wing King Tong Paper Products Co.Ltd. Shenzhen, Guangdong Province, China

Date of Production: September 2023

Run Number: 5033995

Printed and bound in China.

WKT 10 9 8

# CONTENTS

# INTRODUCTION

Hi! I'm Rae Pritchett, and I created this workbook of 95+ games and activities to support your fourth grader's spelling skills. The spelling words and challenges included in this book were specifically designed to keep children ages 9 to 10 engaged for hours!

As a teacher of 20 years, I combined my knowledge of the words fourth graders should learn to spell with fun ways to engage them as they learn.

*The 4th Grade Spelling Workbook* features 180 spelling words that were chosen based on what fourth graders will likely encounter in the world around them. The 18 word lists are organized into 12 subject areas sure to be of interest to your child. Themes range from sports and music to science and math.

Your child will be entertained and challenged by the 95+ spelling games and activities in this workbook. They include word searches, crossword puzzles, tic-tac-toe grids, code games, and more.

Support your child in getting motivated to learn to spell by starting off on the right foot. Take a walk or have a snack before sitting down to do some activities. Your child will be more receptive to learning when you set them up for success!

Let your child know that when you are completing the activities in this book, the goal is to have fun with a purpose! The activities in this workbook are not your typical boring worksheets. They will help your child learn to spell *and* have fun while doing it!

I truly hope that you and your child have as much fun with this workbook as I had in creating it.

Now let's get spelling!

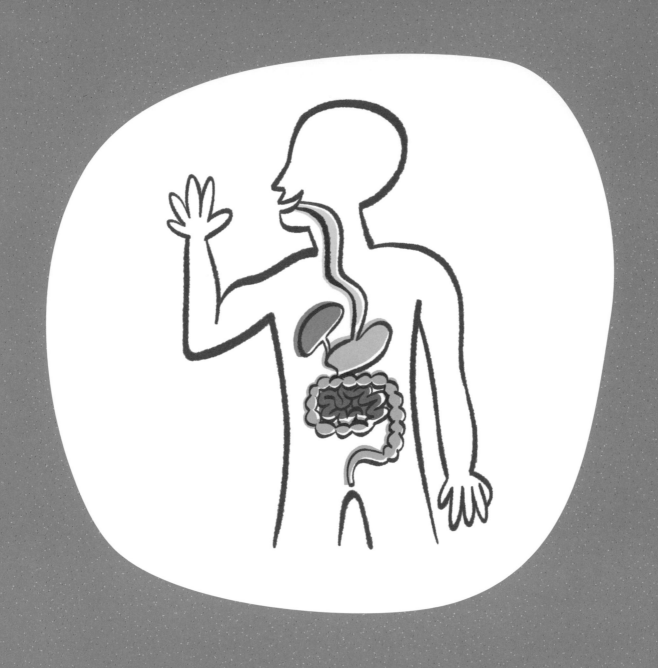

# Words to Learn: ANATOMY WORDS

Write each word in the blank.

1. jaw _____

2. wrist _____

3. ankle _____

4. lungs _____

5. fever _____

6. brain _____

7. bone _____

8. doctor _____

9. surgeon _____

10. skeleton _____

Write your hardest words again here:

_____

_____

# Sick Day

Dustin feels sick. He wants to send his doctor an email. Help him finish his message by using the words from the box to fill in the missing words.

| | | | | |
|---|---|---|---|---|
| lungs | fever | brain | surgeon | doctor |

Dear _____,

I do not feel well. I am stuffy! When I breathe, my

_____ hurt. I have a _____

of 101 degrees. I think my _____ might be

on fire! Do you think I need to see a _____?

Thank you!

Dustin

# Word Search

Circle each word from the list that you find in the word search. Words may go up, down, across, or diagonally, both backward and forward. Write each word as you find it.

| T | S | I | R | W | V | S | S | B | J | R | C |
|---|---|---|---|---|---|---|---|---|---|---|---|
| E | Q | G | J | R | M | K | G | O | A | G | C |
| H | L | A | V | Z | T | E | N | E | X | Z | I |
| I | D | K | Q | T | L | L | U | N | O | J | W |
| E | I | O | N | P | X | E | L | O | M | Z | P |
| I | E | C | C | A | D | T | W | B | L | R | X |
| W | D | F | I | T | T | O | P | M | E | Z | C |
| U | H | L | G | V | O | N | F | V | I | R | M |
| E | G | S | T | O | N | R | E | W | M | V | D |
| S | I | C | U | U | A | F | B | R | A | I | N |
| N | O | E | G | R | U | S | V | Z | S | J | E |
| H | L | T | S | D | K | D | P | O | P | G | O |

jaw _____     brain _____

wrist _____     bone _____

ankle _____     doctor _____

lungs _____     surgeon _____

fever _____     skeleton _____

# Anatomy Word Sort

Sort the words in the box by writing them under the correct category.

| jaw | wrist |
|-----|-------|
| ankle | bone |
| lungs | brain |
| doctor | surgeon |

| BODY PARTS | PEOPLE WHO FIX BODY PARTS |
|------------|---------------------------|
|            |                           |

# Scrambles

Unscramble each set of letters and write the correct spelling words in the blanks.

1. a l e k n _____

2. k s t l e e o n _____

3. e e v f r _____

4. i t w s r _____

5. u r s o n e g _____

6. a b n i r _____

7. e o n b _____

Write a sentence using one of these words.

_____

_____

# Bubbles

Color in the bubbles you need to spell each word from the box.
Unscramble the leftover bubbles to answer the question below.
Write the word in the blank.

| jaw | wrist | ankle | bone |
|-----|-------|-------|------|

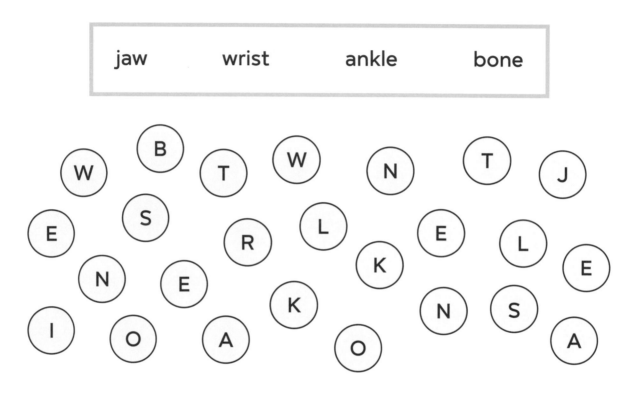

What do all of these body parts make up?

_____

# Words to Learn: MORE ANATOMY WORDS

Write each word in the blank.

1. thumb _____

2. mouth _____

3. stomach _____

4. health _____

5. muscle _____

6. digest _____

7. sneeze _____

8. cough _____

9. hospital _____

10. medicine _____

Write your hardest words again here:

_____

_____

# Crisscross

Choose two anatomy words from the box for each crisscross puzzle. (Hint: Use words that share the same letter.) Write the words in the puzzle. Write the words again on the lines below each puzzle.

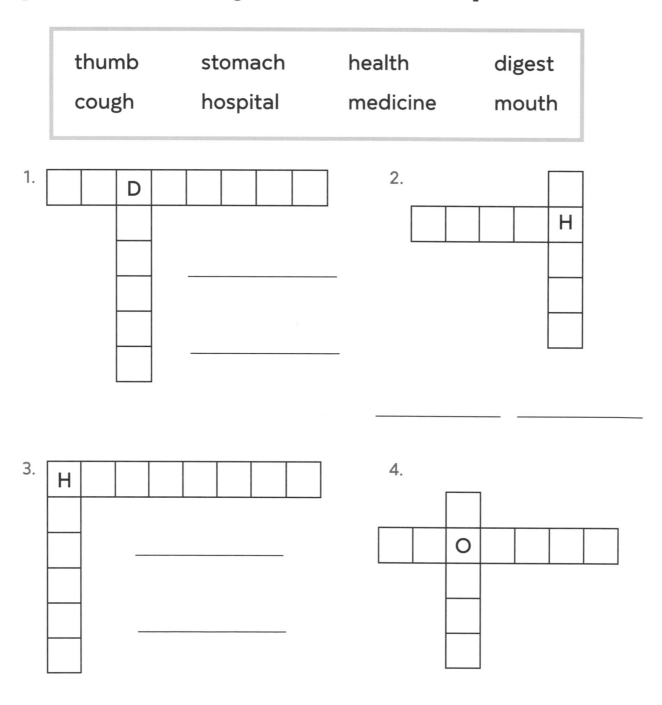

thumb      stomach      health      digest

cough      hospital      medicine      mouth

# ABC Order

Circle the first letter of each word in the box. Write all six words in ABC order in the blanks.

| thumb | health | muscle | digest | sneeze | cough |

1. _____

2. _____

3. _____

4. _____

5. _____

6. _____

# Word Match

Write the letter for each spelling word from the box in front of the correct meaning. Write the spelling word in the blank at the end. Use the letters to fill in the last blank and answer the question below!

| | | |
|---|---|---|
| **A.** digest | **H.** muscle | **T.** sneeze |
| **L.** hospital | **E.** thumb | **H.** mouth |

1. ___ Parts of the human body made of special tissue that helps body parts move _____

2. ___ The short, thick first finger on a human hand _____

3. ___ When food breaks down in the body _____

4. ___ A place where sick or hurt people go to get medical help _____

5. ___ To let out an unexpected burst of air through your mouth and nose _____

6. ___ The part of a person's face that opens and closes for eating, breathing, and speaking _____

What is important for us to take care of?

Our ___ ___ ___ ___ ___ ___

# Tic-Tac-Toe

Circle every word that is spelled correctly. Draw a line across three of them to score a tic-tac-anatomy. Write the misspelled words correctly in the blanks, then use one in a sentence.

| | | |
|---|---|---|
| musle | digest | coff |
| hospital | mouth | health |
| sneze | thum | stomak |

_____

_____

_____

_____

**PUZZLE 10**

# Circle Time

In each line, circle the first, third, fifth, and seventh letters, and so on. Write the circled letters on the first blank to find one anatomy word. Write the leftover letters on the second blank to find another anatomy word.

1. s c n o e u e g z h e

   _____

   _____

2. d m i o g u e t s h t

   _____

   _____

3. h t e h a u l m t b h

   _____

   _____

4. m h e o d s i p c i i t n a e l

   _____

   _____

Write a sentence using one pair of words listed above.

_____

_____

## Words to Learn: NATURE WORDS

Write each word in the blank.

1. cactus   _____

2. humid   _____

3. polar   _____

4. grove   _____

5. prairie   _____

6. garden   _____

7. bloom   _____

8. horizon   _____

9. planet   _____

10. volcano   _____

Write your hardest words again here:

_____

_____

# Write a Poem

Finish this rhyming poem. Use one of the spelling words from the box in each blank. Optional: Draw a picture to go with your poem on another piece of paper.

| cactus | polar | garden | prairie | horizon |
|---|---|---|---|---|

The bees buzz among the flowers in the _____ .

The deer hides in the grass of the _____

as the sun peaks above the _____ .

The _____ bear trudges through the snow.

And the _____ stands tall, looking to the

sun to grow.

**PUZZLE 12**

# Scrambles

Unscramble each set of letters and write the correct spelling words in the blanks.

1. z o r i h o n _____

2. v g r o e _____

3. l n t e p a _____

4. m h i d u _____

5. s a c t c u _____

6. n o c a o l v _____

Write a sentence using one of these words.

_____

_____

# Broken Words

When Zoe tripped, her words fell on the floor and broke apart! Help Zoe rebuild her words by drawing a line from one part to the other part to make a real word. Write the word on the line.

cac      lar      _____

plan      mid      _____

gar      et      _____

po      tus      _____

hu      den      _____

Write a sentence using one of the words listed above.

_____

_____

# Word Search

Circle each nature word from the list that you find in the word search. Words may go up, down, across, or diagonally, both backward and forward. Write each word as you find it.

| D | P | V | S | U | T | C | A | C | J | N | G |
|---|---|---|---|---|---|---|---|---|---|---|---|
| I | I | R | Z | N | R | F | Q | Z | E | Y | R |
| E | F | M | A | I | O | T | G | D | B | R | O |
| K | G | R | U | I | J | Z | R | Z | V | A | V |
| W | E | L | O | H | R | A | I | S | K | L | E |
| B | L | O | O | M | G | I | P | R | Y | O | R |
| S | T | M | Q | J | X | L | E | V | O | P | G |
| M | U | K | O | N | A | C | L | O | V | H | E |
| R | S | X | P | N | A | N | N | R | I | R | Y |
| L | R | A | E | W | T | B | Q | W | I | S | F |
| L | J | T | W | J | J | J | X | U | S | D | W |
| L | D | R | F | I | E | U | R | V | T | G | Z |

cactus _____       garden _____

humid _____       bloom _____

polar _____       grove _____

planet _____       prairie _____

volcano _____       horizon _____

# Word Match

Write the letter for each spelling word from the box in front of the correct meaning. Write the spelling word in the blank at the end. Use the letters to answer the question below!

| | | |
|---|---|---|
| **R.** cactus | **E.** polar | **V.** planet |
| **O.** humid | **G.** volcano | |

1. ___ An opening in the Earth's crust where lava, volcanic ash, and gases escape _____

2. ___ A thick-stemmed, often prickly plant that grows in hot, dry areas _____

3. ___ When there is a lot of water vapor in the air, it feels damp and hot _____

4. ___ The largest object in the solar system after the Sun _____

5. ___ Of or having to do with the North Pole or South Pole of the Earth _____

What is another name for an orchard? ___ ___ ___ ___ ___

# Words to Learn: MORE NATURE WORDS

Write each word in the blank.

1. blizzard _____

2. island _____

3. mountain _____

4. climate _____

5. weather _____

6. hurricane _____

7. tornado _____

8. glacier _____

9. thunder _____

10. rain forest _____

Write your hardest words again here:

_____

_____

# Crossword

Add each of your spelling words to this puzzle. Use the letters that are shown to help you. Cross off each word after you put it into the puzzle. Write each word again on the blank line.

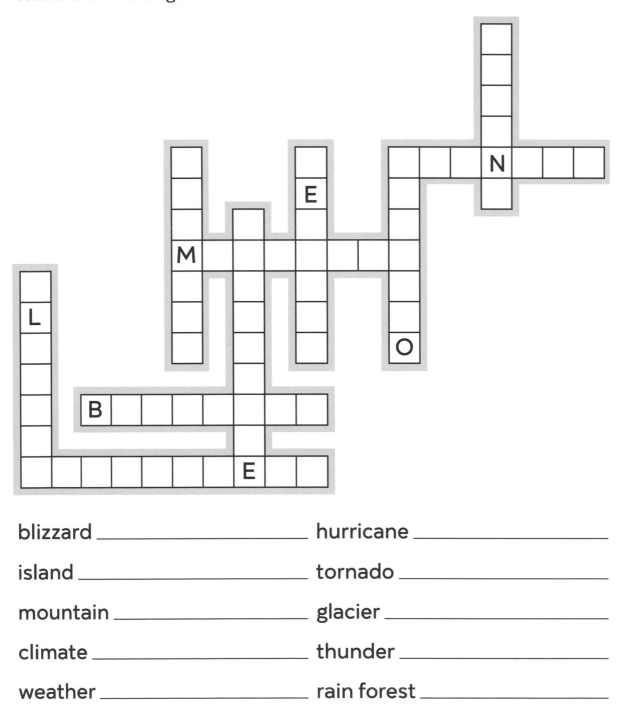

blizzard _____     hurricane _____

island _____     tornado _____

mountain _____     glacier _____

climate _____     thunder _____

weather _____     rain forest _____

# Nature's Connect Four

Can you find four landforms in the puzzle to connect four in a row? Look across, down, and diagonally to find four landforms that connect to solve the puzzle. Draw a line to connect them. Hint: A word may appear more than once.

# Crack the Code

Use the code to find your spelling words. Write each letter as you solve it.

1. 2 ♥ 1 ■ 8 ? 4

——  ——  ——  ——  ——  ——  ——

2. ■ ♥ 8 ● 1 7 ?

——  ——  ——  ——  ——  ——  ——

3. 7 3 4 # 1 5 3

——  ——  ——  ——  ——  ——  ——

4. ● 3 ★ # 7 1 8 #

——  ——  ——  ——  ——  ——  ——  ——

5. ◆ ♥ 8 9 9 1 4 5

——  ——  ——  ——  ——  ——  ——  ——

6. 6 ? 1 7 % ? 4

——  ——  ——  ——  ——  ——  ——

7. 7 % ★ # 5 ? 4

——  ——  ——  ——  ——  ——  ——

| 1 = A | ♥ = L |
|-------|-------|
| 2 = G | ? = E |
| 3 = O | ★ = U |
| 4 = R | ■ = C |
| 5 = D | ◆ = B |
| 6 = W | ● = M |
| 7 = T | # = N |
| 8 = I | % = H |
| 9 = Z | $ = S |

# Nature Word Sort

Write each spelling word in the box under the correct category on the chart.

| blizzard | island |
| mountain | climate |
| hurricane | tornado |
| glacier | thunder |
| rain forest | ocean |

| PLACES YOU CAN GO | WEATHER CONDITIONS |
| --- | --- |
|  |  |

# Write a Story

Add the missing letters to your spelling words so each sentence makes sense. When you have filled in all the missing letters, go back and reread the sentences to read the whole story.

1. Cal went on a cruise to an is ___ ___ ___ ___.

2. The ___ ea ___ ___ ___ ___ was sunny and hot.

3. Cal had read he was traveling to a hot
   ___ ___ i ___ ___ ___ ___.

4. One day, he hiked up a m ___ u ___ t ___ ___ ___.

5. On the last day, Cal was scared because the news said
   the island might have a ___ ur ___ ___ ___ ___ ___ ___.

6. Cal even heard ___ ___ und ___ ___.

7. Cal was happy to go home until he found out that there
   was a bli ___ ___ ard that had hit while he was away!

# Words to Learn: TRAVEL WORDS

Write each word in the blank.

1. explore _____

2. train _____

3. airplane _____

4. conductor _____

5. compass _____

6. pilot _____

7. sailor _____

8. visit _____

9. bridge _____

10. cruise _____

Write your hardest words again here:

_____

_____

# Word Shapes

Write each word from the list into a matching word shape box. The shape of each word must match the shape of the box.

train        cruise        visit

airplane        compass        explore

1.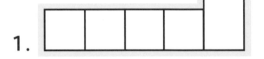

2.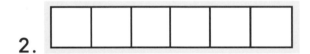

3.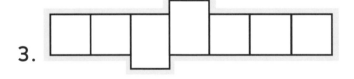

4.

5.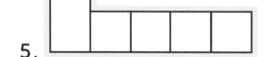

6.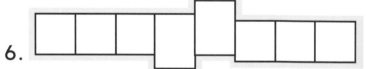

Write a sentence using one of the words listed above.

_____

_____

# Bubbles

Color in the bubbles you need to spell each word from the box. Unscramble the leftover bubbles to answer the question below. Write the word in the blank.

| pilot | train | bridge | cruise |
|-------|-------|--------|--------|

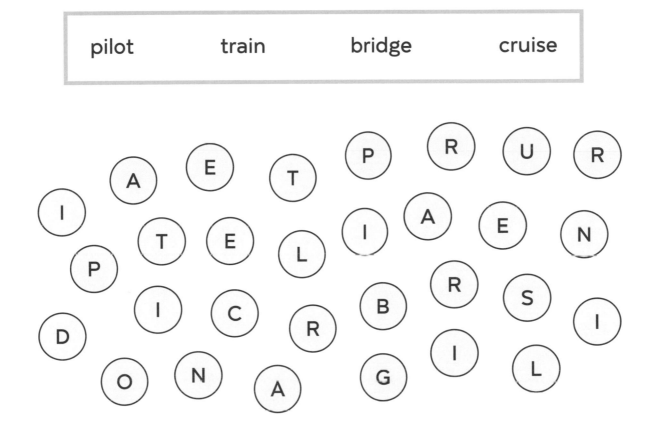

What type of transportation can take you to a place far away?

_____

# Merry-Go-Round

Start at any letter and move around the circle, either forward or backward, to find one of your spelling words. Circle the first letter of the word you find. Write the word under the circle.

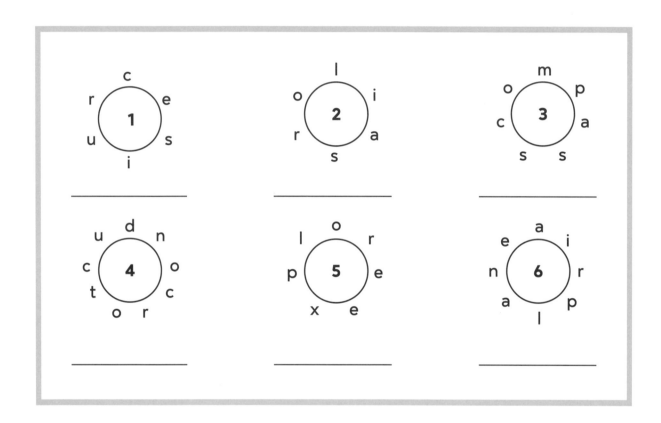

Write a sentence using one of the merry-go-round words.

_____

_____

**PUZZLE 24**

# ABC Order

Circle the first letter of each word in the box. Write all six words in ABC order in the blanks.

conductor  train  explore  airplane  bridge  sailor

1. _____

2. _____

3. _____

4. _____

5. _____

6. _____

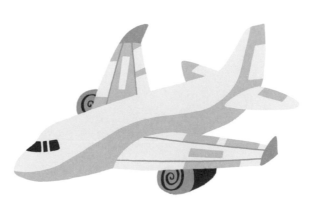

# A Travel Story

Read the story. Choose the correct word to fill in each blank and write it on the line. Optional: Draw a picture of the story on another piece of paper.

Layla loves to _____ (**compass / visit**) new

places. She loves meeting new people and getting to

_____ (**explore / bridge**) different cities. Her

favorite way to travel is by _____ (**bridge / train**).

After she gives her ticket to the _____

(**conductor / pilot**), she finds herself a window seat. She loves

to look out the window, especially when the train goes over

a high _____ (**cruise / bridge**). One day, Layla

hopes to fly on an _____ (**cruise / airplane**),

too. Then Layla will be able to explore even more of the world!

# Words to Learn: MORE TRAVEL WORDS

Write each word in the blank.

1. postcard _____

2. guest _____

3. voyage _____

4. vacation _____

5. adventure _____

6. journey _____

7. tourist _____

8. passport _____

9. suitcase _____

10. luggage _____

Write your hardest words again here:

_____

_____

# Word Search

Circle each word from the list that you find in the word search. Words may go up, down, across, or diagonally, both backward and forward. Write each word as you find it.

| D | U | G | N | I | X | N | Q | Y | Y | E | P |
|---|---|---|---|---|---|---|---|---|---|---|---|
| E | G | A | Y | O | V | U | E | F | S | G | O |
| R | P | V | Y | Y | I | N | W | B | S | A | S |
| U | A | T | M | P | R | T | T | K | M | G | T |
| T | S | P | H | U | Q | I | A | X | R | G | C |
| N | S | O | O | U | Z | D | P | C | U | U | A |
| E | P | J | I | P | K | M | E | E | A | L | R |
| V | O | T | O | U | R | I | S | T | X | V | D |
| D | R | E | C | N | S | T | L | R | E | Q | Y |
| A | T | I | O | D | N | K | Y | E | X | U | B |
| L | N | K | J | G | V | R | Q | V | S | N | Z |
| E | S | A | C | T | I | U | S | Z | L | Y | R |

postcard _____     journey _____

guest _____     tourist _____

voyage _____     passport _____

vacation _____     suitcase _____

adventure _____     luggage _____

# Word Match

Write the letter for each spelling word from the box in front of the correct meaning. Write the spelling word in the blank at the end. Use the letters to fill in the last blank and answer the question below!

| | | |
|---|---|---|
| **G.** suitcase | **A.** vacation | **V.** journey |
| **Y.** adventure | **O.** guest | **E.** postcard |

1. ____ A long trip from one place to another _____

2. ____ A person who pays to stay at a place for the lodging, food, or entertainment it provides _____

3. ____ A journey or activity that is dangerous or exciting

   _____

4. ____ A period of rest from school, work, or other activities

   _____

5. ____ A case used for carrying clothes during travel

   _____

6. ____ A small card often mailed without an envelope

   _____

What is a long journey by air, land, sea, or outer space?

___ ___ ___ ___ ___ ___

# Scrambles

Unscramble each set of letters and write the correct spelling words in the blanks.

1. g a u l g e g _____

2. n o a c a v i t _____

3. s p r o t a d c _____

4. v a t r n d e u e _____

5. p s r o s p a t _____

6. g e o y v a _____

7. t u s r i t o _____

Write a sentence using one of these words.

_____

_____

# Crossword

Add each of your spelling words to this puzzle. Use the letters that are shown to help you. Cross off each word after you put it into the puzzle. Write each word again on the blank line.

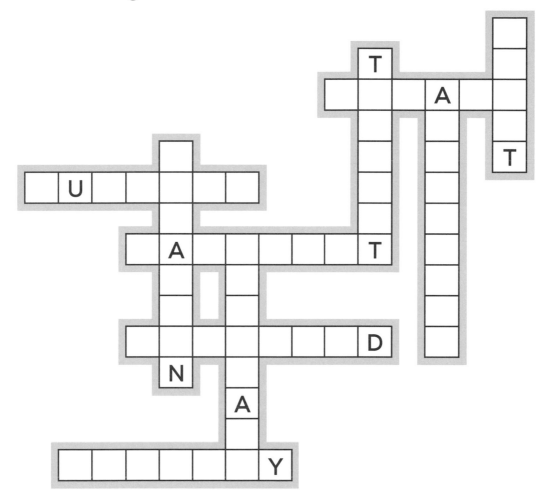

postcard _____    journey _____

guest _____    tourist _____

voyage _____    passport _____

vacation _____    suitcase _____

adventure _____    luggage _____

# Tic-Tac-Toe

Circle every word that is spelled correctly. Draw a line across three of them to score a tic-tac-travel. Write the misspelled words correctly in the blanks, then use one in a sentence.

| | | |
|---|---|---|
| torist | journey | gest |
| adventure | suitcase | vacashun |
| lugage | voyage | postcard |

_____

_____

_____

_____

# Words to Learn: AT HOME WORDS

Write each word in the blank.

1. porch        _____

2. stairs       _____

3. office       _____

4. kitchen      _____

5. microwave    _____

6. faucet       _____

7. furniture    _____

8. blanket      _____

9. towel        _____

10. garage      _____

Write your hardest words again here:

_____

_____

# Crisscross

Choose two spelling words from the box for each crisscross puzzle. (Hint: Use words that share the same letter.) Write the words in the puzzle. Write the words again on the lines below each puzzle.

| office | towel | stairs | furniture |
| kitchen | garage | faucet | microwave |

1.

U

_____  _____

2.

W

_____  _____

3.

E

_____  _____

4.

T

_____  _____

# Bubbles

Color in the bubbles you need to spell each word from the box. Unscramble the leftover bubbles to answer the question below. Write the word in the blank.

| blanket | towel | stairs | faucet |

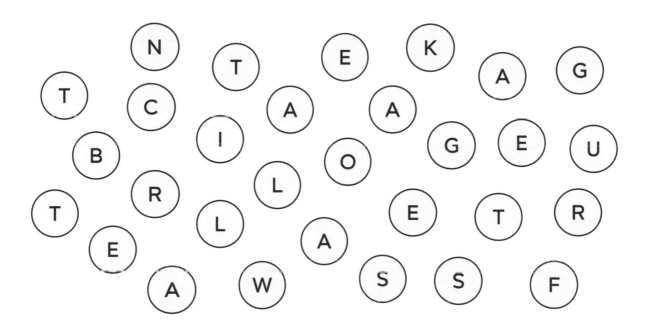

**Where does a person keep their car?**

_____

# Circle Time

In each line, circle the first, third, fifth, and seventh letters, and so on. Write the circled letters on the first blank to find one at-home word. Write the leftover letters on the second blank to find another at-home word.

1. o t f o f w i e c l e

   _____

   _____

2. m f i u c r r n o i w t a u v r e e

   _____

   _____

3. b k l i a t n c k h e e t n

   _____

   _____

4. s g t a a r i a r g s e

   _____

   _____

Write a sentence using one pair of words listed above.

_____

_____

# My House!

Ari's teacher asked him to write about his favorite room in his house. He finished his first draft. Help him complete his final draft by choosing from the words below to fill in the missing words.

| | | | |
|---|---|---|---|
| office | faucet | kitchen | microwave |
| porch | towel | garage | |

My house is white with a red _____. You can get into my house through the front door or through the door in the _____, where our car is parked.

If you go through the garage door, you walk into my favorite room in my house. I go there to cook my favorite foods in the _____.

One time, I made a huge mess, but my sink saved me! It has a long _____ so I could spray the water at my mess. I had to be quiet because my mom was working in her _____, next to the kitchen. I was able to dry it all up with a kitchen _____ before my mom came out for dinner.

Can you guess what my favorite room is? It's the _____!

# Merry-Go-Round

Start at any letter and move around the circle, either forward or backward, to find one of your spelling words. Circle the first letter of the word you find. Write the word under the circle.

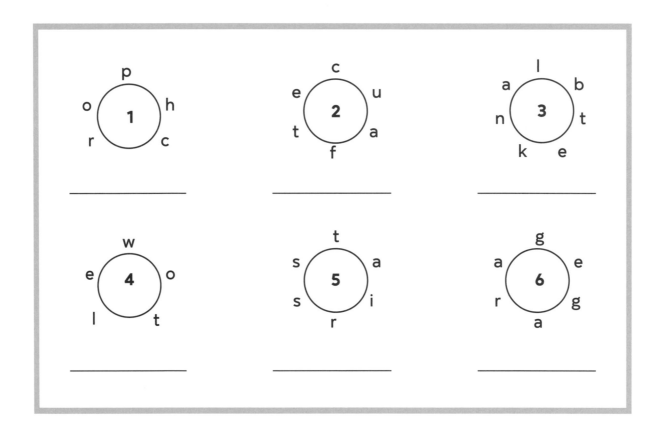

Write a sentence using one of the merry-go-round words.

_____

_____

## Words to Learn: COOKING WORDS

Write each word in the blank.

1. simmer _____

2. recipe _____

3. pour _____

4. blend _____

5. whisk _____

6. marinate _____

7. scramble _____

8. flour _____

9. measure _____

10. spatula _____

Write your hardest words again here:

_____

_____

# Word Search

Circle each word from the list that you find in the word search. Words may go up, down, across, or diagonally, both backward and forward. Write each word as you find it.

| K | R | I | U | Y | F | J | D | E | V | E | R |
|---|---|---|---|---|---|---|---|---|---|---|---|
| S | C | R | A | M | B | L | E | N | T | B | C |
| I | M | Y | D | K | K | X | O | A | E | F | C |
| H | E | S | U | P | P | F | N | U | P | L | S |
| W | A | I | S | Z | K | I | G | R | R | P | B |
| R | S | M | O | E | R | T | E | N | A | M | G |
| Q | U | M | B | A | O | C | R | T | D | D | X |
| Y | R | E | M | O | I | H | U | L | B | R | X |
| R | E | R | U | P | R | L | Y | S | Q | F | P |
| A | F | I | E | N | A | I | C | G | X | E | B |
| R | U | O | P | E | R | M | G | J | J | O | X |
| E | U | Y | H | E | A | T | J | R | Y | N | B |

simmer _____  marinate _____

recipe _____  scramble _____

pour _____  flour _____

blend _____  measure _____

whisk _____  spatula _____

# Crossword

Add each of your spelling words to this puzzle. Use the letters that are shown to help you. Cross off each word after you put it into the puzzle. Write each word again on the blank line.

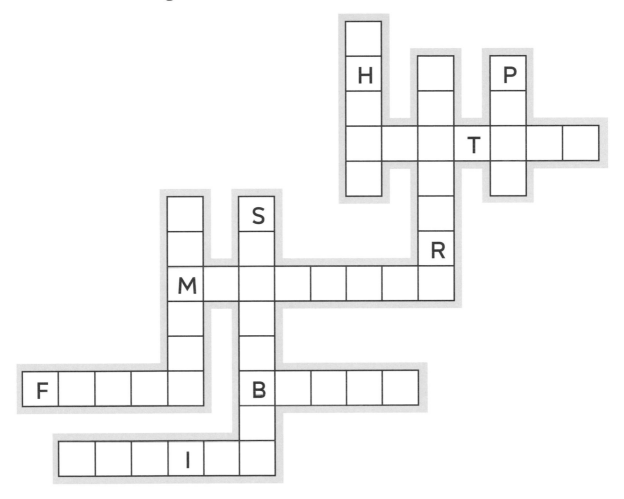

simmer _____     marinate _____

recipe _____     scramble _____

pour _____       flour _____

blend _____      measure _____

whisk _____      spatula _____

# ABC Order

Circle the first letter of each word in the box. Write all six words in ABC order in the blanks.

pour   spatula   blend   simmer   recipe   measure

1. _____

2. _____

3. _____

4. _____

5. _____

6. _____

# Scrambles

Unscramble each set of letters and write the correct spelling words in the blanks.

1. r e a b c m l s _____

2. k i h s w _____

3. u l r o f _____

4. a u l a t p s _____

5. p i e r c e _____

6. e a u m r s e _____

7. m r m i s e _____

Write a sentence using one of these words.

_____

_____

# Recipe Fill-in-the-Blank

Maya found an old family recipe. It's so old that some of the words are hard to see. Help Maya finish the recipe by choosing from the words below to fill in the missing words.

| | | |
|---|---|---|
| scramble | blend | pour |
| whisk | recipe | spatula |

This is a _____ for scrambled eggs. Get a bowl.

Crack an egg. Add some milk. Use a _____ to

_____ the ingredients in the bowl. Then

_____ the ingredients into a pan. Cook on medium

heat. Use a _____ to _____ the eggs as

they cook.

# Words to Learn: MEASUREMENT WORDS

Write each word in the blank.

1. ruler _____

2. protractor _____

3. estimate _____

4. width _____

5. length _____

6. meter _____

7. centimeter _____

8. kilometer _____

9. millimeter _____

10. measurement _____

Write your hardest words again here:

_____

_____

# Crack the Code

Use the code to find your spelling words. Write each letter as you solve it.

1. 4 ★ 9 ? 4

___ ___ ___ ___ ___

2. ♥ 8 9 9 8 ♥ ? 2 ? 4

___ ___ ___ ___ ___ ___ ___ ___ ___ ___

3. ? $ 2 8 ♥ 1 2 ?

___ ___ ___ ___ ___ ___ ___ ___

4. 6 ? ■ 2 8 ♥ ? 2 ? 4

___ ___ ___ ___ ___ ___ ___ ___ ___ ___

5. ♥ ? 1 $ ★ 4 ? ♥ ? ■ 2

___ ___ ___ ___ ___ ___ ___ ___ ___ ___ ___

6. 9 ? ■ # 2 7

___ ___ ___ ___ ___ ___

7. % 8 5 2 7

___ ___ ___ ___ ___

| | |
|---|---|
| 1 = A | ♥ = M |
| 2 = T | ? = E |
| 3 = ● | ★ = U |
| 4 = R | ■ = N |
| 5 = D | ◆ = F |
| 6 = C | □ = Y |
| 7 = H | # = G |
| 8 = I | % = W |
| 9 = L | $ = S |

# Measurement Words

Write one word from the box in each blank space. You will not use all of the words.

| | | | |
|---|---|---|---|
| protractor | meter | measurement | kilometer |
| width | ruler | centimeter | length |

1. The student used a _____ to measure the desk.

2. The _____ is the measurement for how long something is.

3. The _____ is the measurement for how wide something is.

4. When you want to know the length of something, you take a _____.

5. Ben used the _____ to measure the angle.

Write a sentence using one of the leftover measurement words from the box above.

_____

_____

# Word Search

Circle each word from the list that you find in the word search. Words may go up, down, across, or diagonally, both backward and forward. Write each word as you find it.

| H | K | L | R | H | L | A | F | L | P | I | K |
|---|---|---|---|---|---|---|---|---|---|---|---|
| T | X | C | E | N | T | I | M | E | T | E | R |
| G | X | B | T | V | P | D | X | W | J | Z | P |
| N | B | V | E | K | I | L | I | N | S | R | F |
| E | T | A | M | I | T | S | E | W | O | X | H |
| L | V | F | I | L | S | Z | R | T | Z | M | J |
| F | Z | Q | L | O | Z | E | R | J | L | O | G |
| Y | I | R | L | M | T | A | V | O | Z | S | E |
| O | M | U | I | E | C | Q | K | E | S | E | M |
| K | F | L | M | T | U | A | H | N | Y | N | F |
| A | T | E | O | E | Y | N | M | I | C | V | P |
| H | S | R | O | R | M | Y | E | A | C | Y | F |

ruler _____    meter _____

protractor _____    centimeter _____

estimate _____    kilometer _____

width _____    millimeter _____

length _____

# Tic-Tac-Toe

Circle every word that is spelled correctly. Draw a line across three of them to score a tic-tac-measurement. Write the misspelled words correctly in the blanks, then use one in a sentence.

| | | |
|---|---|---|
| meeter | with | length |
| estimate | millimeter | meazurement |
| kilometer | sentimeter | protractor |

_____

_____

_____

_____

# Word Ladder

Start at the bottom of the word ladder. Use each clue to write the measurement word on the blank spaces. Then, use the word you've written to help you solve the next clue. Climb your way from the bottom to the top!

A unit of length equal to one thousandth of a meter.
Drop /cent/.

—— —— —— —— —— —— —— —— —— ——

A unit of length equal to one hundredth of a meter.
Drop /kilo/.

—— —— —— —— —— —— —— —— —— ——

A unit of length equal to one thousand meters.
Keep /meter/.

—— —— —— —— —— —— —— —— ——

The basic unit of length in the metric system. Keep the one vowel and use it twice.

—— —— —— —— ——

How long an object is. Keep the digraph /th/.

—— —— —— —— —— ——

How wide an object is. Keep only one of the only consonant letters that is doubled in the word.

—— —— —— —— ——

estimate

## Words to Learn: READING WORDS

Write each word in the blank.

1.  theme _____

2.  inference _____

3.  narrate _____

4.  text _____

5.  myth _____

6.  poem _____

7.  genre _____

8.  drama _____

9.  evidence _____

10. cite _____

Write your hardest words again here:

_____

_____

# Word Match

Write the letter for each spelling word from the box in front of the correct meaning. Write the spelling word in the blank at the end. Use the letters to fill in the blanks below!

> **E.** genre  **T.** myth  **M.** drama  **E.** narrate  **H.** poem

1. ___ Stories that are part of the traditional knowledge of a society, such as how the world was created _____

2. ___ A piece of writing that often rhymes _____

3. ___ A category of writing, such as fiction or poetry

   _____

4. ___ A type of story acted out before an audience

   _____

5. ___ To tell a story out loud _____

The student was able to cite evidence from the text to answer the questions about the story's ___ ___ ___ ___ ___ .

# Scrambles

Unscramble each set of letters and write the correct spelling words in the blanks.

1. h e e m t _____

2. n d v i e e e c _____

3. x t e t _____

4. e f e c r i n e n _____

5. r a t n r e a _____

Write a sentence using one of these words.

_____

_____

# Merry-Go-Round

Start at any letter and move around the circle, either forward or backward, to find one of your spelling words. Circle the first letter of the word you find. Write the word under the circle.

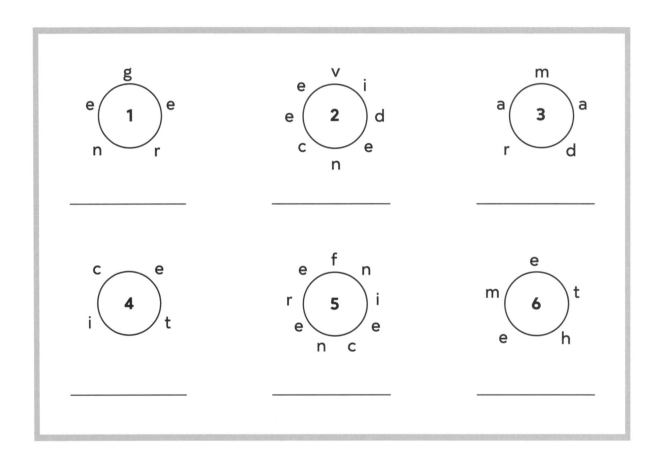

Write a sentence using one of the merry-go-round words.

_____

_____

# Bubbles

Color in the bubbles you need to spell each word from the box. Unscramble the leftover bubbles to answer the question below. Write the word in the blank.

| cite | genre | myth | poem | theme |
|------|-------|------|------|-------|

**What do you need to support your answer?**

_____

# Crisscross

Choose two reading words from the box for each crisscross puzzle. (Hint: Use words that share the same letter.) Write the words in the puzzle. Write the words again on the lines below the puzzle.

| myth | drama | narrate | evidence |
| genre | poem | inference | text |

1.

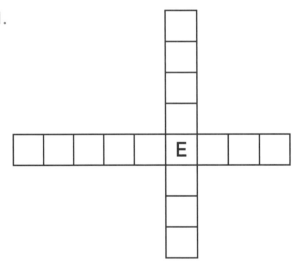

_____  _____

2.

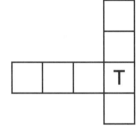

_____  _____

3.

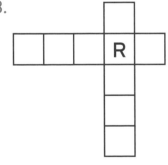

_____  _____

4.

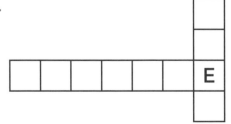

_____  _____

## Words to Learn: MUSIC WORDS

Write each word in the blank.

1. listen  _____

2. audio  _____

3. record  _____

4. headphones  _____

5. violin  _____

6. guitar  _____

7. bass  _____

8. musical  _____

9. vocals  _____

10. microphone  _____

Write your hardest words again here:

_____

_____

# ABC Order

Circle the first letter of each word in the box. Write all six words in ABC order in the blanks.

| violin | guitar | audio | vocals | musical | bass |

1. _____

2. _____

3. _____

4. _____

5. _____

6. _____

# Circle Time

In each line, circle the first, third, fifth, and seventh letters, and so on. Write the circled letters on the first blank to find one music word. Write the leftover letters on the second blank to find another music word.

1. l r i e s c t o e r n d

   _____

   _____

2. h m e i a c d r p o h p o h n o e n s e

   _____

   _____

3. g v u o i c t a a l r s

   _____

   _____

4. m v u i s o i l c i a n l

   _____

   _____

Write a sentence using one pair of words listed above.

_____

_____

# Word Search

Circle each word from the list that you find in the word search. Words may go up, down, across, or diagonally, both backward and forward. Write each word as you find it.

| U | H | N | E | F | G | N | U | M | Q | L | S |
|---|---|---|---|---|---|---|---|---|---|---|---|
| O | K | W | Z | O | I | T | X | U | I | E | E |
| D | U | A | D | L | P | N | G | S | L | N | N |
| Y | O | R | O | R | Y | M | T | I | P | O | O |
| T | U | I | X | S | O | E | H | C | B | H | H |
| Q | V | W | H | Y | N | C | W | A | S | P | P |
| G | U | I | T | A | R | B | E | L | A | O | D |
| S | L | A | C | O | V | X | A | R | A | R | A |
| A | Q | Q | O | I | D | U | A | S | Y | C | E |
| E | L | X | F | A | R | K | M | A | S | I | H |
| H | Y | X | D | P | M | A | A | A | K | M | Y |
| X | B | O | C | M | Q | L | I | E | U | C | Z |

listen _____  guitar _____

audio _____  bass _____

record _____  musical _____

headphones _____  vocals _____

violin _____  microphone _____

# A Music Story

Read the story. Choose the correctly spelled word to fill in each blank and write it on the line. Optional: Draw a picture of the story on another piece of paper.

Ashwin, Emmet, and Hani are in a band. They all have

_____ (**musicle / musical**) talent. Ashwin is

the singer. He can harmonize his _____

(**vocals / voacals**) with different instruments. Emmet plays

the _____ (**basse / bass**) _____

(**gutar / guitar**). Hani plays the _____

(**vyolin / violin**). Their classmates love to _____

(**listen / lissen**) to their music. Maybe one day the band will

_____ (**record / rekord**) an album.

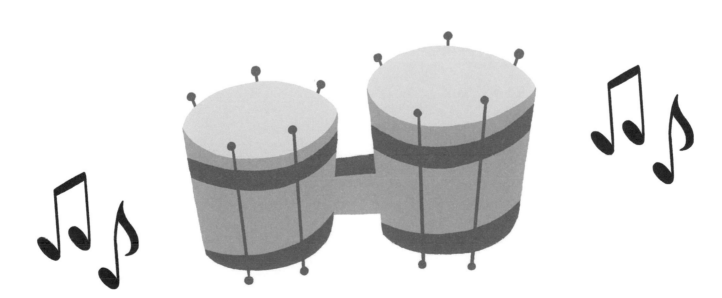

# Crossword

Add each of your spelling words to this puzzle. Use the letters that are shown to help you. Cross off each word after you put it into the puzzle. Write each word again on the blank line.

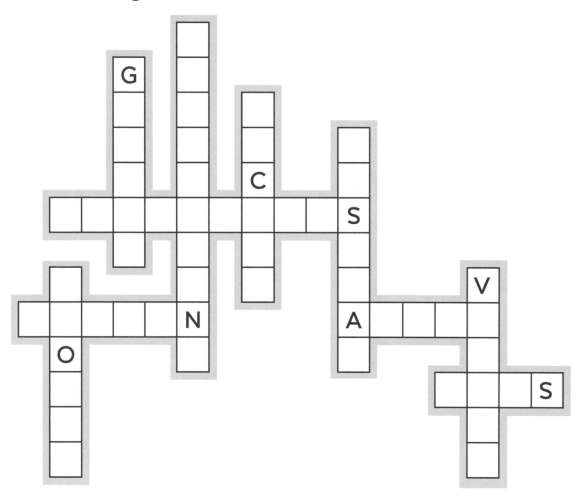

listen _____    guitar _____

audio _____    bass _____

record _____    musical _____

headphones _____    vocals _____

violin _____    microphone _____

# Words to Learn: CELEBRATION WORDS

Write each word in the blank.

1. parade _____

2. carnival _____

3. festival _____

4. festivities _____

5. firecrackers _____

6. fireworks _____

7. surprise _____

8. present _____

9. celebrate _____

10. celebration _____

Write your hardest words again here:

_____

_____

# Word Ladder

Start at the bottom of the word ladder. Use each clue to write the measurement word on the blank spaces. Then, use the word you've written to help you solve the next clue. Climb your way from the bottom to the top!

The act of celebrating. Keep the first seven letters.

__ __ __ __ __ __ __ __ __ __

To honor someone. Keep one consonant /c/.

__ __ __ __ __ __ __ __ __

Devices that make a loud noise when exploded. Keep /fire/.

__ __ __ __ __ __ __ __ __ __

Devices that burn or explode to make noise, bright lights, or brilliant colors. Keep the first consonant /f/ and the last /s/.

__ __ __ __ __ __ __ __ __

Events planned for a celebration. Keep the first six letters.

__ __ __ __ __ __ __ __ __ __ __

festival

# Word Search

Circle each word from the list that you find in the word search. Words may go up, down, across, or diagonally, both backward and forward. Write each word as you find it.

| C | A | R | N | I | V | A | L | G | N | F | E |
|---|---|---|---|---|---|---|---|---|---|---|---|
| S | X | F | L | F | N | C | T | P | O | E | S |
| G | K | J | E | S | M | R | L | T | I | S | I |
| Q | A | R | G | S | E | S | N | R | T | T | R |
| N | R | J | O | D | T | E | W | I | A | I | P |
| S | S | E | A | W | S | I | H | I | R | V | R |
| E | H | R | G | E | E | X | V | F | B | I | U |
| V | A | Z | R | Z | D | R | V | A | E | T | S |
| P | Q | P | Y | P | E | H | I | S | L | I | M |
| H | P | L | S | S | S | F | L | F | E | E | ^ |
| C | E | L | E | B | R | A | T | E | C | S | J |
| S | R | E | K | C | A | R | C | E | R | I | F |

parade _____     fireworks _____

carnival _____     surprise _____

festival _____     present _____

festivities _____     celebrate _____

firecrackers _____     celebration _____

# Word Match

Write the letter for each spelling word from the box in front of the correct meaning. Write the spelling word in the blank at the end. Use the letters to fill in the last blank and answer the question below!

| | | |
|---|---|---|
| **D.** surprise | **A.** present | **P.** festival |
| **A.** celebrate | **R.** firecrackers | **E.** carnival |

1. ___ A ceremony or celebration that involves special activities or amusements _____

2. ___ A gift _____

3. ___ Devices that make a loud noise when exploded _____

4. ___ To honor something or someone with a party or presents _____

5. ___ An unexpected event _____

6. ___ A traveling enterprise of amusements like rides, contests, and food _____

What is a celebration that usually consists of marching bands and vehicles in front of spectators? ___ ___ ___ ___ ___ ___

**PUZZLE 59**

# Bubbles

Color in the bubbles you need to spell each word from the box. Unscramble the leftover bubbles to answer the question below. Write the word in the blank.

| carnival | present | celebration |
|----------|---------|-------------|

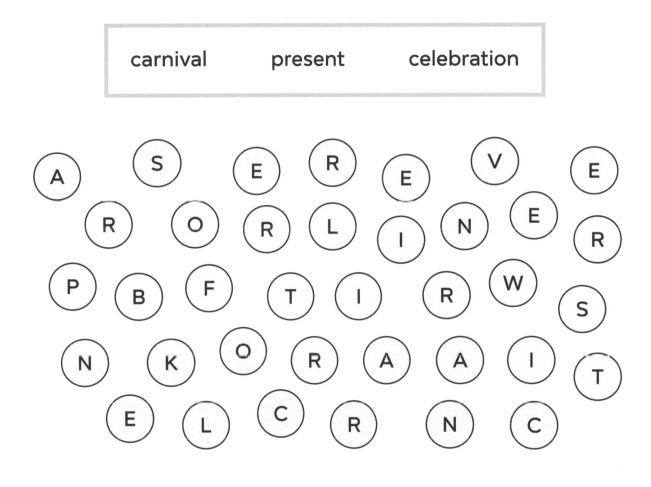

What devices make a loud noise when they explode?

_____

# Merry-Go-Round

Start at any letter and move around the circle, either forward or backward, to find one of your spelling words. Circle the first letter of the word you find. Write the word under the circle.

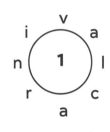

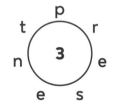

_____

_____

_____

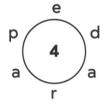

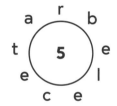

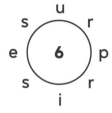

_____

_____

_____

Write a sentence using one of the merry-go-round words.

_____

_____

# Words to Learn: SPORTS WORDS

Write each word in the blank.

1. league  _____

2. victory  _____

3. stadium  _____

4. court  _____

5. helmet  _____

6. athlete  _____

7. coach  _____

8. basketball  _____

9. softball  _____

10. tennis  _____

Write your hardest words again here:

_____

_____

# Circle Time

In each line, circle the first, third, fifth, and seventh letters, and so on. Write the circled letters on the first blank to find one sports word. Write the leftover letters on the second blank to find another sports word.

1. c c o o u a r c t h

   _____

   _____

2. l h e e a l g m u e e t

   _____

   _____

3. s v t i a c d t i o u r m y

   _____

   _____

4. a t t e h n l n e i t s e

   _____

   _____

Write a sentence using one pair of words listed above.

_____

_____

# Crack the Code

Use the code to find your spelling words. Write each letter as you solve it.

1. % ? ♥ ● ? 7

    — — — — — —

2. ★ 1 4 ◆ ? 7 ★ 1 ♥ ♥

    — — — — — — — — — —

3. 2 3 1 2 %

    — — — — —

4. 7 ? ■ ■ 8 4

    — — — — — —

5. 4 7 1 5 8 # ●

    — — — — — — —

6. 4 3 9 7 ★ 1 ♥ ♥

    — — — — — — — —

7. 2 3 # 6 7

    — — — — —

| | |
|---|---|
| 1 = A | ♥ = L |
| 2 = C | ? = E |
| 3 = O | ★ = B |
| 4 = S | ■ = N |
| 5 = D | ◆ = K |
| 6 = R | ● = M |
| 7 = T | # = U |
| 8 = I | % = H |
| 9 = F | |

# Crisscross

Choose two sports words from the box for each crisscross puzzle. (Hint: Use words that share the same letter.) Write the words in the puzzle. Write the words again on the lines below the puzzle.

| tennis | athlete | basketball | league |
| softball | coach | court | victory |

1.

I

_____  _____

2.

T

_____  _____

3.

A

_____  _____

4.

T

_____  _____

# Tic-Tac-Toe

Circle every word that is spelled correctly. Draw a line across three of them to score a tic-tac-sports. Write the misspelled words correctly in the blanks, then use one in a sentence.

| | | |
|---|---|---|
| cort | athleet | helmut |
| coach | sofball | league |
| tennis | victory | stadium |

_____

_____

_____

_____

# Word Ladder

Start at the bottom of the word ladder. Use each clue to write the measurement word on the blank spaces. Then, use the word you've written to help you solve the next clue. Climb your way from the bottom to the top!

A word that starts with the same first letter /c/, but means a person who directs, instructs, and trains an athlete.

___ ___ ___ ___ ___

A quadrilateral area marked for ball games. Keep one /t/.

___ ___ ___ ___ ___

A seven-letter word for a person who plays sports. Keep the consonant /t/ and one /l/.

___ ___ ___ ___ ___ ___ ___

A modified form of baseball played on a smaller field with a larger ball, seven rather than nine innings, and underarm pitching. Keep the word /ball/.

___ ___ ___ ___ ___ ___ ___ ___ ___

basketball

# Words to Learn: MORE SPORTS WORDS

Write each word in the blank.

1. practice _____

2. referee _____

3. goalie _____

4. hockey _____

5. volleyball _____

6. overtime _____

7. halftime _____

8. gymnasium _____

9. tournament _____

10. championship _____

Write your hardest words again here:

_____

_____

# Sophia's Volleyball Journal

Sophia writes about her volleyball practices and her games in her volleyball journal. Choose the correctly spelled word to fill in each blank and write it on the line. Optional: Draw a picture of Sophia's entry on another piece of paper.

I had _____ (**practis / practice**) today. It was

raining outside, so we met in the _____

(**gymnasium / gymnazeum**). The other team does not come

to our practice, so we do not need a _____

(**refree / referee**). Coach gave us a pep talk before the

_____ (**tournament / turnament**) on

Saturday. If we win this game, we go on to the

_____ (**chamonship/ championship**) game.

And if we win the tournament, that means we will have more

_____ (**volleeball / volleyball**) practices.

# ABC Order

Circle the first letter of each word in the box. Write all six words in ABC order in the blanks.

| | | |
|---|---|---|
| practice | referee | hockey |
| volleyball | gymnasium | championship |

1. _____

2. _____

3. _____

4. _____

5. _____

6. _____

# Circle Time

In each line, circle the first, third, fifth, and seventh letters, and so on. Write the circled letters on the first blank to find one spelling word. Write the leftover letters on the second blank to find another spelling word.

1. o h v a e l r f t t i i m m e e

   _____

   _____

2. r h e o f c e k r e e y e

   _____

   _____

3. v t o o l u l r e n y a b m a e l n l t

   _____

   _____

Write a sentence using one pair of words listed above.

_____

_____

# Crossword

Add each of your spelling words to this puzzle. Use the letters that are shown to help you. Cross off each word after you put it into the puzzle. Write each word again in the blank space.

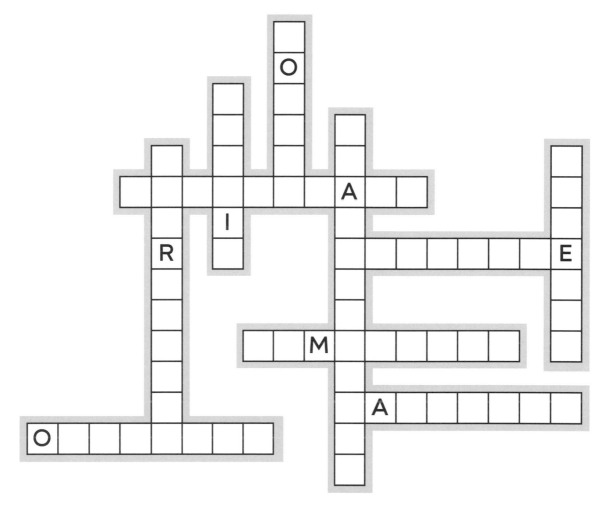

practice _____        overtime _____

referee _____        halftime _____

goalie _____        gymnasium _____

hockey _____        tournament _____

volleyball _____        championship _____

# Crack the Code

Use the code to find your spelling words. Write each letter as you solve it.

1. 9 5 7 ● # 1

—— —— —— —— —— ——

2. ◆ 5 2 ■ % #

—— —— —— —— —— ——

3. 9 2 ■ 4 ? % 8 #

—— —— —— —— —— —— —— ——

4. 5 6 # 3 ? % 8 #

—— —— —— —— —— —— —— ——

5. 3 # 4 # 3 # #

—— —— —— —— —— —— ——

6. ◆ 1 8 + 2 ★ % ♥ 8

—— —— —— —— —— —— —— —— ——

7. ? 5 ♥ 3 + 2 8 # + ?

—— —— —— —— —— —— —— —— —— ——

| 1 = Y | ♥ = U |
|---|---|
| 2 = A | ? = T |
| 3 = R | ★ = S |
| 4 = F | ■ = L |
| 5 = O | ◆ = G |
| 6 = V | ● = K |
| 7 = C | # = E |
| 8 = M | % = I |
| 9 = H | + = N |

## Words to Learn: FEELINGS WORDS

Write each word in the blank.

1. calm _____

2. anxiety _____

3. resolve _____

4. argue _____

5. fight _____

6. fear _____

7. agree _____

8. agreement _____

9. disagree _____

10. disagreement _____

Write your hardest words again here:

_____

_____

# Word Match

Write the letter for each spelling word from the box to give the antonym (a word having the opposite meaning) or the synonym (a word having the same meaning) of the given word. Use the letters to answer the question below!

| | | | |
|---|---|---|---|
| **L.** disagreement | **C.** agree | **M.** anxiety | **A.** afraid |

1. ___ What word is an antonym for disagree? _____

2. ___ What word is a synonym for fear? _____

3. ___ What word is an antonym for agreement?

   _____

4. ___ What word is a synonym for feelings of fear, dread, and uneasiness that may happen as a reaction to stress? _____

Which of your spelling words is a synonym for a feeling of being at peace?

___ ___ ___ ___

# Word Search

Circle each word from the list that you find in the word search. Words may go up, down, across, or diagonally, both backward and forward. Write each word as you find it.

| T | Y | Y | X | K | B | P | A | E | X | H | A |
|---|---|---|---|---|---|---|---|---|---|---|---|
| N | H | T | T | F | E | H | S | E | J | K | F |
| E | D | X | E | B | L | T | C | R | F | E | R |
| M | L | A | C | I | E | Q | M | G | H | V | Q |
| E | J | F | H | U | X | Z | W | A | Y | L | D |
| E | Y | G | G | J | G | N | G | S | H | O | A |
| R | S | R | T | Y | W | Q | A | I | V | S | G |
| G | A | S | V | U | C | G | V | D | B | E | R |
| A | E | G | Q | F | O | A | A | U | R | E |
| S | F | I | G | H | T | E | I | T | L | D | E |
| I | C | K | H | Q | N | B | A | D | K | Z | R |
| D | P | T | N | E | M | E | E | R | G | A | Z |

anxiety _____    fight _____

argue _____    agree _____

resolve _____    agreement _____

fear _____    disagree _____

calm _____    disagreement _____

# Scrambles

Unscramble each set of letters and write the correct spelling words in the blanks.

1. e s d e g i a r _____

2. t y n i a x e _____

3. t f h i g _____

4. e v o l r e s _____

5. n e e r m a e t g _____

Write a sentence using one of these spelling words.

_____

_____

# Crisscross

Choose two feelings words from the box for each crisscross puzzle. (Hint: Use words that share the same letter.) Write the words in the puzzle. Write the words again on the lines below the puzzle.

| fight | resolve | agree | disagree |
| fear | argue | agreement | anxiety |

1.

F

2.

E

_____  _____

_____  _____

3.

E

4.

E

_____  _____

_____  _____

# Merry-Go-Round

Start at any letter and move around the circle, either forward or backward, to find one of your spelling words. Circle the first letter of the word you find. Write the word under the circle.

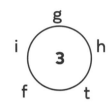

_____

_____

_____

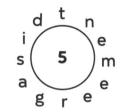

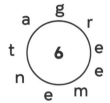

_____

_____

_____

Write a sentence using one of the merry-go-round words.

_____

_____

# Words to Learn: MORE FEELINGS

Write each word in the blank.

1. emotion _____

2. happier _____

3. happiest _____

4. happiness _____

5. angrier _____

6. angriest _____

7. angriness _____

8. peace _____

9. peaceful _____

10. peacefully _____

Write your hardest words again here:

_____

_____

# Word Match

Which suffix fits? Add a suffix from the box to each word to spell it correctly and finish the sentences. Use the letters to fill in the missing spelling word in the positive affirmation below!

| **E.** -iest | **P.** -ly | **A.** -ier | **C.** -ful |
|---|---|---|---|

1. ___ They acted peaceful _____

2. ___ Giselle was the angr_____ she had ever been.

3. ___ Jorge was happ_____ than before.

4. ___ They looked so peace_____ while they slept.

5. ___ Rosalie was the happi_____ when her parents

   sat in the front of the audience.

I feel at ___ ___ ___ ___ ___ when I am calm.

# Crossword

Add each of your spelling words to this puzzle. Use the letters that are shown to help you. Cross off each word after you put it into the puzzle. Write each word again in the blank space.

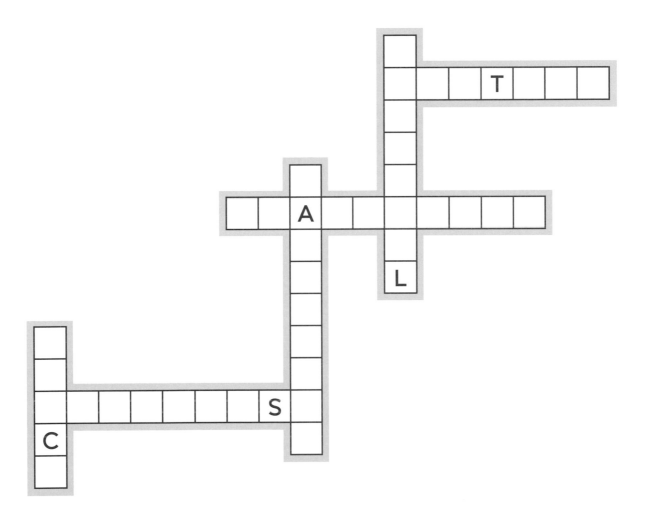

emotion _____        happiness _____

peaceful _____        peace _____

peacefully _____        angriness _____

# Bubbles

Color in the bubbles you need to spell each word from the box. Unscramble the leftover bubbles to fill in the blank to answer the question below. Write the word in the blank.

| emotion | peaceful | peace | happier |

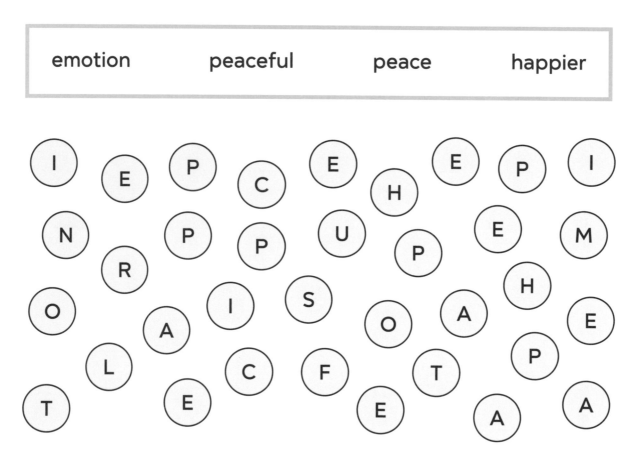

If Aki and Rowan are happy, but Kip is happier than both Aki and Rowan, what does that make Kip?

Kip is the _____ of the three.

# Word Ladder

Start at the bottom of the word ladder. Use each clue to write the measurement word on the blank spaces. Then, use the word you've written to help you solve the next clue. Climb your way from the bottom to the top!

The most angry. Keep the /iest/.

— — — — — — — —

The most happy. Delete the /r/.

— — — — — — — —

A feeling of joy. Delete the prefix. Change the /y/ to an /i/ and add /er/.

— — — — — — —

The opposite of angriness. Keep the suffix /ness/.

— — — — — — — — —

angriness

# Scrambles

Unscramble each set of letters and write the correct spelling words in the blanks.

1. e e c p a _____

2. n o i t e m o _____

3. e t s i a n g r _____

4. l y p u c e e f l a _____

5. s e n s a p h i p _____

6. a g n r r e i _____

7. u f a c e l e p _____

8. r e h i p p a _____

Write a sentence using one of these words.

_____

_____

# Words to Learn: SCIENCE AND TECHNOLOGY WORDS

Write each word in the blank.

1. gravity _____

2. density _____

3. reaction _____

4. force _____

5. motion _____

6. electricity _____

7. magnet _____

8. circuit _____

9. physical _____

10. chemical _____

Write your hardest words again here:

_____

_____

# Word Match

Write the letter for each spelling word from the box in front of the correct meaning. Write the spelling word in the blank at the end. Use the letters to fill in the last blank and answer the question below!

**E.** density      **N.** force      **A.** motion

**M.** electricity      **T.** reaction      **G.** gravity

1. ___ A form of energy that can give things the ability to move and work _____

2. ___ A change in an object's position _____

3. ___ An invisible force that pulls objects toward each other _____

4. ___ A push or pull on an object _____

5. ___ The state or condition of having parts very close together with little space between _____

6. ___ An action or response to something that has happened or has been done; can be chemical _____

What is an object that has the power to pull items made of iron toward itself?

___ ___ ___ ___ ___ ___

# Tic-Tac-Toe

Circle every word that is spelled correctly. Draw a line across three of them to score a tic-tac-science. Write the misspelled words correctly in the blanks, then use one in a sentence.

| | | |
|---|---|---|
| force | reakshun | physical |
| gravatee | electrisitey | chemical |
| moshun | density | magnet |

_____

_____

_____

_____

# Crisscross

Choose two science and technology words from the box for each crisscross puzzle. (Hint: Use words that share the same letter.) Write the words in the puzzle. Write the words again on the lines below the puzzle.

| force | circuit | chemical | gravity |
|-------|---------|----------|---------|
| motion | magnet | physical | reaction |

1.

C

_____  _____

2.

I

_____  _____

3.

A

_____  _____

4.

C

_____  _____

**PUZZLE 84**

# Science Homework

Help Nissa finish her science homework. Choose the correct word to fill in each blank and write it on the line.

Matter can go through changes. In a _____ (**chemikal / chemical**) change, a new substance is made. Burning a candle is an example of a chemical change. In a _____ (**fisical / physical**) change, no new substance is made. When water turns to ice, there is a physical change. The water changes from a liquid to a solid.

Changes are a _____ (**reeakshun / reaction**), or response to something that has been done to the matter.

An example of a reaction is when an object is moving, or in _____ (**moshun / motion**), and someone pushes the object. The push on the object is called the _____ (**fors / force**). This push makes the object go faster, and going faster is a reaction.

Bonus: Do you know what kind of reaction this is?

_____

# Spelling Spin

Use the tip of a pencil to hold the loop of a paperclip in the center of the circle. Flick the paperclip. Use the letter the paperclip lands on to spell the words below. Keep spinning until you have all of the words spelled correctly.

1. ___ orce

2. ___ ensity

3. ___ lectricity

4. ___ ircuit

5. ___ hemical

6. ___ otion

7. ___ agnet

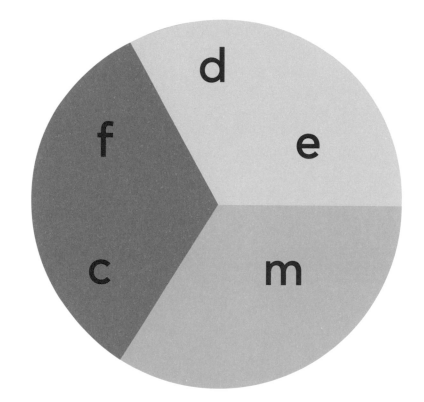

Write a sentence using one of the words listed above.

_____

_____

# Words to Learn: MORE SCIENCE AND TECHNOLOGY WORDS

Write each word in the blank.

1. research _____

2. cycle _____

3. ecosystem _____

4. fossil _____

5. adaptation _____

6. trait _____

7. heredity _____

8. engineer _____

9. technology _____

10. experiment _____

Write your hardest words again here:

_____

_____

# Crack the Code

Use the code to find the spelling word that completes the definition. Write each letter as you solve it.

1. A ♥ 7 ♥ # 2 __C__ __Y__ __C__ __L__ __E__ is a circle of events that repeats in a regular pattern.

2. An 2 ♥ ♦ 5 7 5 ? 2 1

   __E__ __C__ __O__ __S__ __Y__ __S__ __T__ __E__ __M__ is a community of interacting organisms and their environment.

| | | |
|---|---|---|
| 1 = M | 7 = Y | ■ = P |
| 2 = E | 8 = F | ♦ = O |
| 3 = D | 9 = H | □ = D |
| 4 = N | ♥ = C | # = L |
| 5 = S | ? = T | % = I |
| 6 = R | ★ = A | |

3. A 8 ♦ 5 5 % # __F__ __O__ __S__ __S__ __I__ __L__ is the remains or trace of a plant or animal that lived a long time ago.

4. ★ □ ★ ■ ? ★ ? % ♦ 4 __A__ __D__ __A__ __P__ __T__ __A__ __T__ __I__ __O__ __N__ is the natural process where an animal or plant species changes over time to become better suited to its habitat.

5. A ? 6 ★ % ? __T__ __R__ __A__ __I__ __T__ is a physical characteristic like hair color.

6. 9 2 6 2 □ % ? 7 __H__ __E__ __R__ __E__ __D__ __I__ __T__ __Y__ is the passing down of traits like hair or eye color from a parent to a child.

# Scrambles

Unscramble each set of letters and write the correct spelling words in the blanks.

1. s i o f s l _____

2. r e e n i e g n _____

3. h g l t e o y c n o _____

4. e p m e i n x e t r _____

5. d t e i y r h e _____

6. n o a p i a d t a t _____

7. y e o m s t c s e _____

Write a sentence using one of these words.

_____

_____

# ABC Order

Circle the first letter of each word in the box. Write all six words in ABC order in the blanks.

| | | |
|---|---|---|
| heredity | adaptation | trait |
| fossil | cycle | engineer |

1. _____

2. _____

3. _____

4. _____

5. _____

6. _____

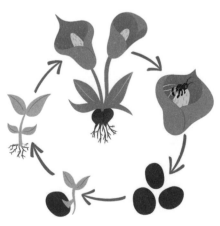

# Word Search

Circle each science and technology word from the list that you find in the word search. Words may go up, down, across, or diagonally, both backward and forward. Write each word as you find it.

| R | A | Q | V | R | F | F | U | O | T | U | E |
|---|---|---|---|---|---|---|---|---|---|---|---|
| P | N | C | L | V | E | S | F | I | Z | C | W |
| H | O | O | K | K | Q | S | A | R | O | L | O |
| L | I | S | S | O | F | R | E | S | H | Y | O |
| L | T | E | A | E | T | E | Y | A | K | C | L |
| W | A | N | T | L | R | S | R | B | R | R | T |
| M | T | G | D | N | T | E | F | J | W | C | A |
| C | P | I | F | E | Z | O | P | M | Y | C | H |
| Y | A | N | M | H | E | R | E | D | I | T | Y |
| C | D | E | X | P | E | R | I | M | E | N | T |
| L | A | E | E | X | W | U | I | L | Z | F | P |
| E | B | R | V | C | T | L | S | P | K | S | T |

research _____     trait _____

cycle _____     heredity _____

ecosystem _____     engineer _____

fossil _____     experiment _____

adaptation _____

# Crisscross

Choose two science and technology words from the box for each crisscross puzzle. (Hint: Use words that share the same letter.) Write the words in the puzzle. Write the words again on the lines below the puzzle.

| research | trait | experiment | cycle |
|----------|-------|------------|-------|
| engineer | heredity | ecosystem | technology |

1.

C

_____  _____

2.

T

_____  _____

3.

E

_____

_____

4.

E

_____

_____

**PUZZLE 91**

# Circle Time

In each line, circle the first, third, fifth, and seventh letters, and so on. Write the circled letters on the first blank to find one spelling word. Write the leftover letters on the second blank to find another spelling word. Then write a sentence using the pair of words.

1. e c x o p m l p o a r s e s

   _____     _____

   _____

2. c l i e r n c g u t i h t

   _____     _____

   _____

3. c p e r l a e c b t r i a c t e e

   _____     _____

   _____

4. p d e i a s c a e g f r u e l e

   _____     _____

   _____

PUZZLE 92

# Scrambles

Unscramble each set of letters and write the correct spelling words in the blanks. Then write a sentence for each word.

1. l s a i h p o t _____

   _____

2. z z d l a i b r _____

   _____

3. y o h e n g l t c o _____

   _____

4. e e e f e r r _____

   _____

5. e c u s i r _____

   _____

6. e e e n z s _____

   _____

**PUZZLE 93**

# Bubbles

Color in the bubbles you need to spell each word from the box.
Unscramble the leftover bubbles to answer the question below.
Write the word in the blank.

| surgeon | sailor | coach |
|---------|--------|-------|
| bone | reaction | |

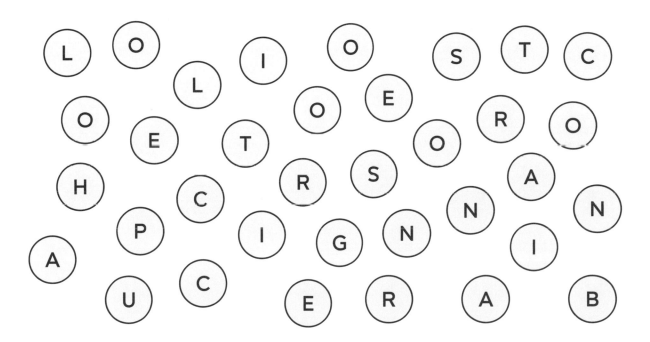

**What is the name of the person who flies an airplane?**

_____

**PUZZLE 94**

# My School Day!

Kalina's teacher asked her to write about her day at school. She finished her first draft. Help her complete her final draft by circling the correctly spelled word and writing it on the line.

I woke up for school in a bad mood. I got _____ (**happier / happyer**) when I remembered that the _____ (**muzical / musical**) was today. Plus, it was the last day before _____ (**vacation / vacashun**). This made me feel _____ (**kalm / calm**). In the morning, I had English class. We were learning about _____ (**genra / genre**). In class, I raised my hand to read the _____ (**poem / poim**). After English, I had math. We worked on _____ (**mezurement / measurement**). We measured the length and the _____ (**with / width**) of our classroom. In science, we had an _____ (**engineer / enjinere**) speak to our class about an _____ (**eksperiment / experiment**) he was working on. Then, at the end of the day, we had the musical! It was great!

## PUZZLE 95

# Crossword

Add each of your spelling words to this puzzle. Use the letters that are shown to help you. Cross off each word after you put it into the puzzle. Write each word again in the blank space.

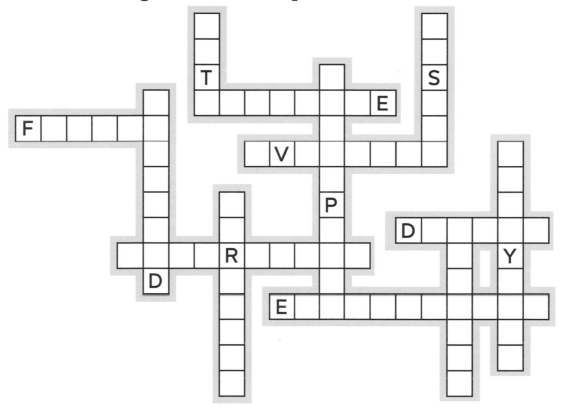

halftime _____

overtime _____

microphone _____

marinate _____

myth _____

fossil _____

electricity _____

muscle _____

digest _____

ecosystem _____

glacier _____

protractor _____

**PUZZLE 96**

# Word Search

Circle each spelling word from the list that you find in the word search. Words may go up, down, across, or diagonally, both backward and forward. Write each word as you find it.

| L | Q | U | N | N | W | E | G | M | Q | P | V |
|---|---|---|---|---|---|---|---|---|---|---|---|
| E | P | G | R | J | E | H | P | U | L | J | I |
| M | D | E | T | X | A | T | T | I | A | O | D |
| O | E | P | C | F | T | C | W | D | C | G | Y |
| T | F | D | W | N | H | Q | E | A | U | E | C |
| I | P | G | I | Y | E | S | E | T | W | L | R |
| O | F | I | P | C | R | D | D | S | I | B | W |
| N | V | A | I | A | I | R | I | M | M | U | E |
| H | E | A | L | T | H | N | A | V | Y | H | S |
| Y | B | R | J | T | R | T | E | Q | E | J | H |
| W | T | N | E | M | E | R | U | S | A | E | M |
| N | O | I | T | A | C | A | V | Q | O | H | A |

health _____    recipe _____

medicine _____    measurement _____

weather _____    evidence _____

climate _____    stadium _____

vacation _____    emotion _____

PUZZLE 97

# Crack the Code

Crack this code to read a secret message! Use the code to find your spelling words. Write each letter as you solve it.

2 ♥ ● 9 ● ? 2 ★ _ _ _ _ _ _ _ _! You have finished all

of the activities! What ★ 8 % 6 ? % ■ _ _ _ _ _ _ _ are

you feeling? You should 4 ★ 1 ★ 5 ● # 6 ★ _ _ _ _ _ _ _ _ _

with a 9 # ● # 7 ★ _ _ _ _ _ _. This means that you

can spell 180 words! You should be the ◆ # 9 9 ? ★ 2 6

_ _ _ _ _ _ _ _ person in the room right now!

Take a minute to have a 4 ★ 1 ★ 5 ● # 6 ? % ■

_ _ _ _ _ _ _ _ _ _ _. Congratulations!

You are amazing!

| | | |
|---|---|---|
| 1 = L | 7 = D | ■ = N |
| 2 = S | 8 = M | ◆ = H |
| 3 = F | 9 = P | ● = R |
| 4 = C | ♥ = U | # = A |
| 5 = B | ? = I | % = O |
| 6 = T | ★ = E | |

# ANSWER KEY

## PUZZLE 1

doctor

lungs

fever

brain

surgeon

## PUZZLE 2

| T | S | I | R | W | V | S | S | B | J | R | C |
|---|---|---|---|---|---|---|---|---|---|---|---|
| E | Q | G | J | R | M | K | G | O | A | G | C |
| H | L | A | V | Z | T | E | N | E | X | Z | I |
| I | D | K | Q | T | L | L | U | N | O | J | W |
| E | I | O | N | P | X | E | L | O | M | Z | P |
| I | E | C | C | A | D | T | W | B | L | R | X |
| W | D | F | I | T | T | O | P | M | E | Z | C |
| U | H | L | G | V | O | N | F | V | I | R | M |
| E | G | S | T | O | N | R | E | W | M | V | D |
| S | I | C | U | U | A | F | B | R | A | I | N |
| N | O | E | G | R | U | S | V | Z | S | J | E |
| H | L | T | S | D | K | D | P | O | P | G | O |

## PUZZLE 3

| Body Parts | People Who Fix Body Parts |
|---|---|
| jaw<br>wrist<br>ankle<br>lungs<br>bone<br>brain | surgeon<br>doctor |

## PUZZLE 4

1. ankle
2. skeleton
3. fever
4. wrist
5. surgeon
6. brain
7. bone

Sentences will vary.

## PUZZLE 5

SKELETON

## PUZZLE 6

1. medicine/digest
2. mouth/thumb
3. health/hospital
4. stomach/cough

## PUZZLE 7

1. cough
2. digest
3. health
4. muscle
5. sneeze
6. thumb

## PUZZLE 8

1. H, muscle
2. E, thumb
3. A, digest
4. L, hospital
5. T, sneeze
6. H, mouth

HEALTH

## PUZZLE 9

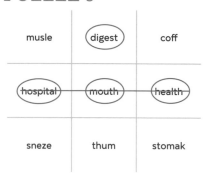

Corrections: muscle, cough, sneeze, thumb, stomach
Sentences will vary.

## PUZZLE 10

1. sneeze/cough
2. digest/mouth
3. health/thumb
4. medicine/hospital

Sentences will vary.

## PUZZLE 11

garden

prairie

horizon

polar

cactus

## PUZZLE 12

1. horizon
2. grove
3. planet
4. humid
5. cactus
6. volcano

Sentences will vary.

## PUZZLE 13

cactus

planet

garden

polar

humid

Sentences will vary.

## PUZZLE 14

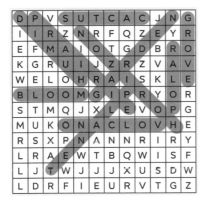

## PUZZLE 15

1. G, volcano
2. R, cactus
3. O, humid
4. V, planet
5. E, polar

GROVE

## PUZZLE 16

## PUZZLE 17

| blizzard | tornado | climate | mountain |
|----------|---------|----------|-------------|
| island | thunder | hurricane | weather |
| weather | glacier | weather | rain forest |
| ~~island~~ | ~~desert~~ | ~~mountain~~ | ~~glacier~~ |

## PUZZLE 18

1. glacier
2. climate
3. tornado
4. mountain
5. blizzard
6. weather
7. thunder

## PUZZLE 19

| Places You Can Go | Weather Conditions |
|-------------------|--------------------|
| island | blizzard |
| mountain | climate |
| glacier | hurricane |
| ocean | tornado |
| rain forest | thunder |

## PUZZLE 20

1. island
2. weather
3. climate
4. mountain
5. hurricane
6. thunder
7. blizzard

## PUZZLE 21

1. visit
2. cruise
3. explore
4. compass
5. train
6. airplane

Sentences will vary.

## PUZZLE 22

AIRPLANE

## PUZZLE 23

1. cruise
2. sailor
3. compass
4. conductor
5. explore
6. airplane

Sentences will vary.

## PUZZLE 24

1. airplane
2. bridge
3. conductor
4. explore
5. sailor
6. train

## PUZZLE 25

visit

explore

train

conductor

bridge

airplane

## PUZZLE 26

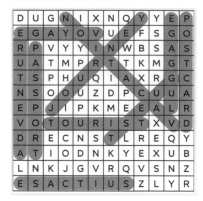

## PUZZLE 27

1. V, journey
2. O, guest
3. Y, adventure
4. A, vacation
5. G, suitcase
6. E, postcard

VOYAGE

## PUZZLE 28

1. luggage
2. vacation
3. postcard
4. adventure
5. passport
6. voyage
7. tourist

Sentences will vary.

## PUZZLE 29

## PUZZLE 30

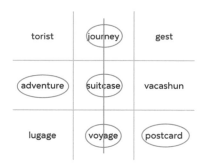

Corrections: tourist, guest, vacation, luggage
Sentences will vary.

## PUZZLE 31

1. furniture/faucet
2. microwave/towel
3. garage/office
4. stairs/kitchen

## PUZZLE 32

GARAGE

## PUZZLE 33

1. office/towel
2. microwave/furniture
3. blanket/kitchen
4. stairs/garage

Sentences will vary.

## PUZZLE 34

porch

garage

microwave

faucet

office

towel

kitchen

## PUZZLE 35

1. porch
2. faucet
3. blanket
4. towel
5. stairs
6. garage

Sentences will vary.

## PUZZLE 36

## PUZZLE 37

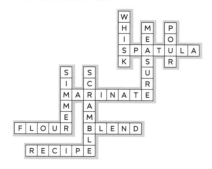

## PUZZLE 38

1. blend
2. measure
3. pour
4. recipe
5. simmer
6. spatula

## PUZZLE 39

1. scramble
2. whisk
3. flour
4. spatula
5. recipe
6. measure
7. simmer

## PUZZLE 40

recipe

whisk

blend

pour

spatula

scramble

## PUZZLE 41

1. ruler
2. millimeter
3. estimate
4. centimeter
5. measurement
6. length
7. width

## PUZZLE 42

1. ruler
2. length
3. width
4. measurement
5. protractor

Sentence answers will vary.

## PUZZLE 43

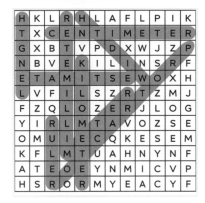

## PUZZLE 44

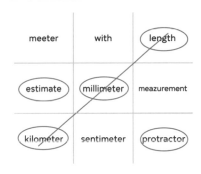

Corrections: meter, width, measurement, centimeter
Sentences will vary.

## PUZZLE 45

millimeter

centimeter

kilometer

meter

length

width

## PUZZLE 46

1. T, myth
2. H, poem
3. E, genre
4. M, drama
5. E, narrate

THEME

## PUZZLE 47

1. theme
2. evidence
3. text
4. inference
5. narrate

Sentences will vary.

## PUZZLE 48

1. genre
2. evidence
3. drama
4. cite
5. inference
6. theme

Sentences will vary.

## PUZZLE 49

EVIDENCE

## PUZZLE 50

1. inference/evidence
2. text/myth
3. genre/drama
4. poem/narrate

## PUZZLE 51

1. audio
2. bass
3. guitar
4. musical
5. violin
6. vocals

## PUZZLE 52

1. listen/record
2. headphones/ microphone
3. guitar/vocals
4. musical/violin

Sentences will vary.

## PUZZLE 53

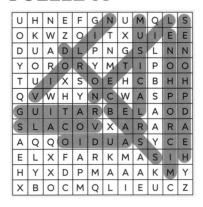

## PUZZLE 54

musical

vocals

bass

guitar

violin

listen

record

## PUZZLE 55

## PUZZLE 56

celebration

celebrate

firecrackers

fireworks

festivities

festival

## PUZZLE 57

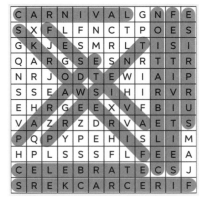

## PUZZLE 58

1. P, festival
2. A, present
3. R, firecrackers
4. A, celebrate
5. D, surprise
6. E, carnival

PARADE

## PUZZLE 59

FIREWORKS

## PUZZLE 60

1. carnival
2. festival
3. present
4. parade
5. celebrate
6. surprise

Sentences will vary.

## PUZZLE 61

1. court/coach
2. league/helmet
3. stadium/victory
4. athlete/tennis

Sentences will vary.

## PUZZLE 62

1. helmet
2. basketball
3. coach
4. tennis
5. stadium
6. softball
7. court

## PUZZLE 63

1. tennis/victory
2. softball/athlete
3. league/coach
4. basketball/court

## PUZZLE 64

| cort | athleet | helmut |
|------|---------|--------|
| (coach) | sofball | (league) |
| (~~tennis~~) | (~~victory~~) | (~~stadium~~) |

Corrections: court, athlete, softball, helmet
Sentences will vary.

## PUZZLE 65

coach

court

athlete

softball

basketball

## PUZZLE 66

practice

gymnasium

referee

tournament

championship

volleyball

## PUZZLE 67

1. championship
2. gymnasium
3. hockey
4. practice
5. referee
6. volleyball

## PUZZLE 68

1. overtime/halftime
2. referee/hockey
3. volleyball/tournament

Sentences will vary.

## PUZZLE 69

## PUZZLE 70

1. hockey
2. goalie
3. halftime
4. overtime
5. referee
6. gymnasium
7. tournament

## PUZZLE 71

1. C, agree
2. A, afraid
3. L, disagreement
4. M, anxiety

CALM

## PUZZLE 72

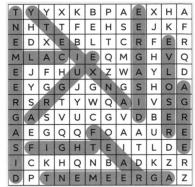

## PUZZLE 73

1. disagree
2. anxiety
3. fight
4. resolve
5. agreement

Sentences will vary.

## PUZZLE 74

1. fight/fear
2. agreement/agree
3. argue/resolve
4. anxiety/disagree

## PUZZLE 75

1. fear
2. resolve
3. fight
4. argue
5. disagreement
6. agreement

Sentences will vary.

## PUZZLE 76

1. P, peacefully
2. E, angriest
3. A, happier
4. C, peaceful
5. E, happiest

PEACE

## PUZZLE 77

## PUZZLE 78

HAPPIEST

## PUZZLE 79

angriest

happiest

happier

happiness

angriness

## PUZZLE 80

1. peace
2. emotion
3. angriest
4. peacefully
5. happiness
6. angrier
7. peaceful
8. happier

Sentences will vary.

## PUZZLE 81

1. M, electricity
2. A, motion
3. G, gravity
4. N, force
5. E, density
6. T, reaction

MAGNET

## PUZZLE 82

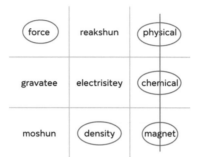

Corrections: gravity, motion, reaction, electricity
Sentences will vary.

## PUZZLE 83

1. reaction/circuit
2. motion/physical
3. magnet/gravity
4. chemical/force

## PUZZLE 84

chemical

physical

reaction

motion

force

Bonus: physical

## PUZZLE 85

1. force
2. density
3. electricity
4. circuit
5. chemical
6. motion
7. magnet

Sentences will vary.

## PUZZLE 86

1. cycle
2. ecosystem
3. fossil
4. adaptation
5. trait
6. heredity

## PUZZLE 87

1. fossil
2. engineer
3. technology
4. experiment
5. heredity
6. adaptation
7. ecosystem

Sentences will vary.

## PUZZLE 88

1. adaptation
2. cycle
3. engineer
4. fossil
5. heredity
6. trait

## PUZZLE 89

```
R A Q V R F F U O T U E
P N C L V E S F I Z C W
H O O K K Q S A R O L O
L I S S O F R E S H Y O
L T E A E T E Y A K C L
W A N T L R S R B R R T
M T G D N T E F J W C A
C P I F E Z O P M Y C H
Y A N M H E R E D I T Y
C D E X P E R I M E N T
L A E E X W U I L Z F P
E B R V C T L S P K S T
```

## PUZZLE 90

1. cycle/research
2. heredity/trait
3. technology/engineer
4. experiment/ecosystem

## PUZZLE 91

1. explore/compass
2. circuit/length
3. celebrate/practice
4. peaceful/disagree

Sentences will vary.

## PUZZLE 92

1. hospital
2. blizzard
3. technology
4. referee
5. cruise
6. sneeze

Sentences will vary.

## PUZZLE 93

PILOT

## PUZZLE 94

happier

musical

vacation

calm

genre

poem

measurement

width

engineer

experiment

## PUZZLE 95

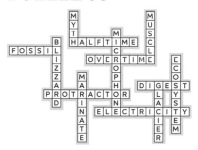

## PUZZLE 96

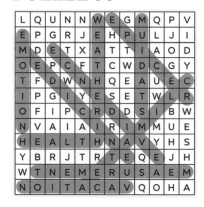

## PUZZLE 97

surprise

emotion

celebrate

parade

happiest

celebration

# ABOUT THE AUTHOR

 **Rae Pritchett** is a curriculum author and teacher specializing in the area of literacy. Rae is a passionate educator with more than 20 years of teaching experience. She loves reading, writing, and researching best practices for teaching. Rae holds a master's degree in education, a Certificate of Advanced Graduate Study in educational leadership, and is a certified dyslexia practitioner. She shares her knowledge on her blog, *Miss Rae's Room* (MissRaesRoom.com). She also teaches education courses through The Learning Tree PDN (TLTPDN.com), an online teaching college Rae co-owns with her teacher husband. In her free time, she enjoys hiking, exploring, and spending time with her family.